THE WITHAM TO MALDON R∤
A pictorial history

CW00394032

FOREWORD

I worked for Marconi's in Chelmsford for 37 years until I retired in 1997 as a Senior Designer.

We moved to Wickham Bishops in 1968, two years after the Witham – Maldon line closed. Driving home from work the country way would take me past Wickham Bishops station, which is about a mile and a half from the centre of the village. One of the trestle bridges can be seen from the road and this prompted me to take a closer look. I made a model of the trestle bridge to a scale of 1:76 (00 scale). Things progressed gradually and it ended up as an 18 foot long model of Wickham Bishops railway station. It is in four sections for transportation, and has been shown at various model railway exhibitions.

The model was featured in a seven-page spread in 'Model Rail', August 2006, and some pictures from it can be seen at the end of the book, courtesy of Martyn Barnwell, Model Rail.

During the 20 years or so it has taken to get to this stage I have acquired many photographs from various sources and much information about the Witham-Maldon line. I thought it would be nice to compile these photos, most of which have not been published before, into a pictorial history of the line.

I hope you enjoy looking at these nostalgic photographs as much as I do.

Len Wilkinson

First published November 2010 / Reprinted April 2011 / October 2011
Copyright Len Wilkinson and Essex Transport Publishing
Designed and published by Essex Transport Publishing
ISBN 9780956683205
British Library Cataloguing in Publication Data
A catalogue record for this book is available from the British Library

Printed by the Crescent Card Company, Tiptree, Colchester, Essex

£4.95

INTRODUCTION

This book is not intended to be a definitive history of the Witham to Maldon railway - this is covered adequately by the booklet 'Branch Lines to Maldon' by the late Dennis Swindale (now in its third edition). Nevertheless, I think a brief history of the line would not go amiss.

The line started off as the Maldon, Witham and Braintree Railway and plans were deposited with the Clerk of the Peace in February 1845. Royal Assent was given on 18th June 1846. Running rights had been given to the Eastern counties Railway, who pledged themselves to open the line within the next eighteen months. Work was started in March 1847 and by May more than 500 men were at work on the line, this number increasing to 1,000 by July. The line was to be double tracked with stations at Wickham (later Wickham Bishops), Langford and Ulting, and a terminus at Maldon on the Witham – Maldon section. In mid-August 1848, goods trains started running and on September 30th, 1848 the line was passed for the conveyance of passengers. The first passenger train left Maldon at 8am on Monday, October 2nd, 1848. The line didn't stay double tracked for long. In 1850 or thereabouts one track was lifted. In 1862 the Eastern Counties Railway was taken over by the Great Eastern Railway.

Maldon Station was renamed Maldon East on 1st October 1889, with the suffix 'and Heybridge' being added from 1st October 1907. With the advent of the 1923 grouping, the branch became part of the London and North Eastern Railway. In 1948, nationalisation arrived and the line became part of the Eastern Region of British Railways. During the fifties, freight traffic increased, outwards traffic being mainly Kingsmere jams, tinned fruit and vegetables from Goldhanger Fruit Farms, also agricultural machinery from Bentalls at Maldon and sugar beet from Wickham Bishops and, at times, peas. Inwards traffic was mainly wheat and seed potatoes for Matthews Mill, brewer's grains for DB Smith, Wickham Hall and road surfacing grit for ECC and coal at Maldon. Some photographs show Witham station as being 'Witham Junction', but it is not known when it became 'Witham Junction' and when it reverted back to plain 'Witham'.

THE RAILBUS ERA

The old steam engines, mainly F5's and J15's were nearing the end of their time. Steam was being phased out rapidly in the Eastern Region, and two-coach diesel sets took their place from June 14th 1956. In April 1958, the Eastern Region were supplied with five railbuses, manufactured by the German firm Waggon und Maschinenbau. Services began on July 7th 1958, but they were not wholly reliable due to mechanical troubles. Also the railbuses couldn't cope with the increasing traffic and were replaced by two and four car diesel sets. The railbuses did carry on until closure to passengers on September 7th 1964.

END OF STEAM AND FINAL DAYS

The last steam hauled goods train pulled out of Maldon East early in 1961. From then on only diesels served the branch. In 1962 the 'Beeching Axe' was happening and, although various campaign committees tried to stimulate opposition to the closure delaying it for several months, on August 11th 1964 the official notification of closure was issued. It stated that the passenger train service between Witham and Maldon would be withdrawn on and from Monday 7th September 1964. So it was then, that on Sunday, September 6th the last diesel set left Maldon for Witham, the return journey being made in near darkness.

FREIGHT ONLY

For the last two years, the Witham to Maldon branch was freight only, carrying mainly canned fruit and agricultural machinery. Soon, with the transportation of large loads of canned fruit by rail diminishing, even the freight service on the Witham to Maldon branch drew to a close. As 1966 came in, it was announced that it was proposed to close Maldon East station Goods in April. The last freight train to leave Maldon East station on April 15th 1966 was hauled by Type 1 Bo-Bo diesel locomotive number D8202. In 1969 the track was removed, finally sealing the fate of the line.

THE LINE SINCE CLOSURE

The course of the line from Witham can be followed up to where a timber viaduct (now demolished) crossed the River Brain. The trackbed can be rejoined and followed up to Blue Mills Road Bridge (demolished in 1977). The next section is all in private ownership.

Wickham Bishops station house is in private ownership, and is now unrecognisable due to numerous extensions, although the platform and the concrete base of the signal box still remain in place. Further down the line, the Mill House by the River Blackwater, although in private hands, is virtually unchanged from the front elevation. The house was originally lived in by the foreman of the line, the single storey section being the stables. The two wooden viaducts at Wickham Bishops were restored in 1995 and are now an Ancient Monument. When the line was singled in the mid-nineteenth century, the viaduct was split down the middle and what remains is the up side. Also, during GER days, the long viaduct was made into two, the centre section between the River Blackwater and the mill cut being turned into an embankment, thus creating two shorter viaducts. The Mill house can be seen from the footpath that runs from the road to the second viaduct that crosses the Mill cut.

The bridge at Langford and Ulting Halt is still there, although filled in underneath. The platform is intact but very overgrown.

From here, the track towards Maldon is quite clear up to the triangular junction. A new road obliterates the last stage, including the signal box, demolished in September 1979. The other side of the site of the level crossing was the large goods shed which has recently been demolished. Maldon East station has been variously a public house, restaurant and a Motel and Nightclub. It is now used as offices.

IMPORTANT DATES IN CHRONOLOGICAL ORDER

1843	Line from Brentwood to Colchester opened.
1848	Maldon, Witham and Braintree Railway opened.
1862	Absorbed into Great Eastern Railway.
1889	Maldon to Woodham Ferrers branch opened.
1905	Accident at Witham (station rebuilt).
1923	Became part of London and North Eastern Railway.
1939	Maldon to Woodham Ferrers branch closed to passengers.

1948	-	Became Eastern Region of British Railways.
1953	-	Maldon to Woodham Ferrers branch closed.
1958	-	Last steam passenger train.
		German railbuses introduced.
1961	-	End of steam on branch.
1964	-	Line closed to passengers.
1966	-	Complete closure.
1969	-	Track removed.

ABOUT THE WICKHAM BISHOPS LAYOUT

The model is a scale replica of Wickham Bishops station area in the late Fifties/early Sixties. The station house, platform, Mill House, road bridge and the trestle bridge were all measured and photographed and the models made to scale. The track is EM gauge, which is the correct four feet eight and a half inches, as opposed to OO gauge. Nearly forty trees plus bushes, grass, etc., make it just like a country station should look like. Steam engines (J15, J69 and F5) were built from kits and diesels include the railbus, class 15 type 1 Bo-Bo and the Class 105 DMU. It is booked for more exhibitions, so maybe I will see you there!

ACKNOWLEDGEMENTS

First of all I would like to thank Mark House for all his hard work in collating all the photographs and information for the book. As I have said in the foreword, many of the photographs have been acquired over a period of twenty years, so I am not sure where some of them came from. Some of the photographs are part of the collection of Frank Church, courtesy of the Essex Bus Enthusiasts Group, some are from the collection of Dr. Paddy Lacey, and some from the Maldon Museum collection.

The credits for the photographs used appear where known, and my thanks go to all those who have contributed, but I must apologise to anyone whose photograph I have used and not accredited.

I would also like to thank my eldest daughter, Sarah, for doing the typing.

Len Wilkinson
August 2010

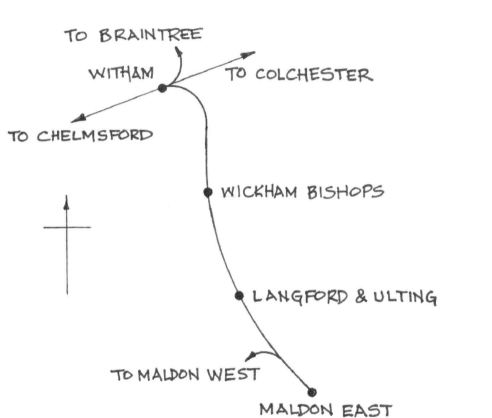

TO BRAINTREE

WITHAM

TO COLCHESTER

TO CHELMSFORD

WICKHAM BISHOPS

LANGFORD & ULTING

TO MALDON WEST

MALDON EAST

THE WITHAM TO MALDON BRANCH

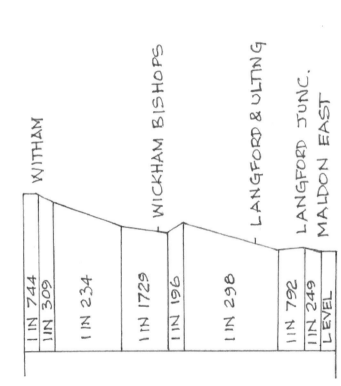

WITHAM

WICKHAM BISHOPS

LANGFORD & ULTING

LANGFORD JUNC.

MALDON EAST

1 IN 744 · 1 IN 309 · 1 IN 234 · 1 IN 1729 · 1 IN 196 · 1 IN 298 · 1 IN 792 · 1 IN 249 · LEVEL

GRADIENT DIAGRAM

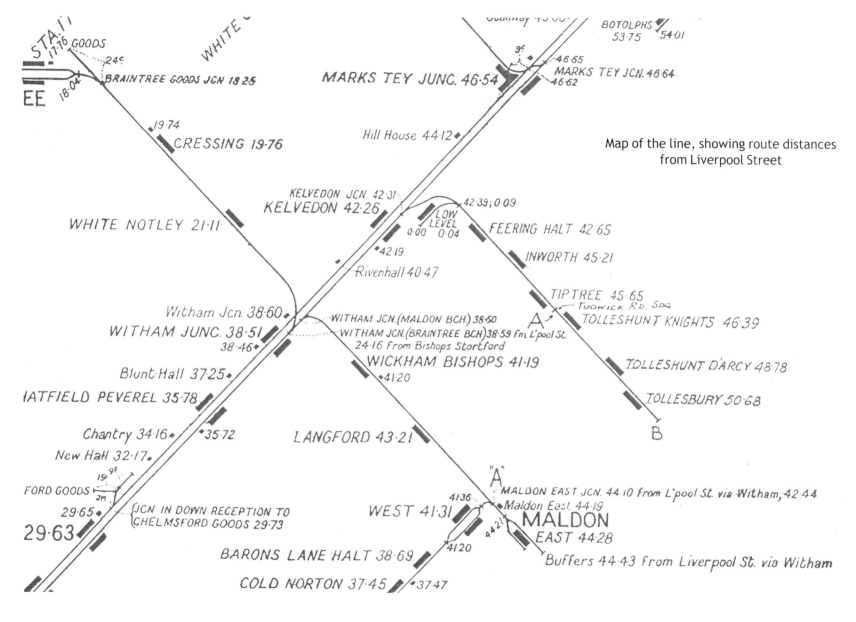

Map of the line, showing route distances from Liverpool Street

STA.T 17·76 GOODS
EE
24°
BRAINTREE GOODS JCN 18·25
18·04
19·74
CRESSING 19·76
WHITE NOTLEY 21·11

WHITE

BOTOLPHS 53·75   54·01
9°
46·65
MARKS TEY JUNC. 46·54   MARKS TEY JCN. 46·64
46·62

Hill House 44·12

KELVEDON JCN. 42·31
KELVEDON 42·26   42·39; 0·09
LOW LEVEL
0·00   0·04
FEERING HALT 42·65
42·19
INWORTH 45·21
Rivenhall 40·47

Witham Jcn. 38·60
WITHAM JUNC. 38·51   WITHAM JCN.(MALDON BCH.) 38·60
38·46   WITHAM JCN.(BRAINTREE BCH) 38·59 fm L'pool St.
24·16 from Bishops Stortford
WICKHAM BISHOPS 41·19
41·20

TIPTREE 45·65
"A"   TUDWICK RD, SDG
TOLLESHUNT KNIGHTS 46·39

TOLLESHUNT D'ARCY 48·78

TOLLESBURY 50·68

B

Blunt Hall 37·25
HATFIELD PEVEREL 35·78
Chantry 34·16   35·72
New Hall 32·17
FORD GOODS   15° 9°
2M
29·65
29·63   JCN. IN DOWN RECEPTION TO
CHELMSFORD GOODS 29·73

LANGFORD 43·21

"A"
MALDON EAST JCN. 44·10 from L'pool St. via Witham, 42·44
41·36   Maldon East 44·19
WEST 41·31   MALDON
44·21   EAST 44·28
41·20
BARONS LANE HALT 38·69
COLD NORTON 37·45   37·47
Buffers 44·43 from Liverpool St. via Witham

Witham goods yard and the ECR goods shed in 1911 looking north eastward, with the water tower and signal box. The Maldon branch to right, Braintree branch to left. (Photograph courtesy of the Historical Model Railway Society)

B12 1542 heading a Down express through Witham Junction in 1947. The road bridge in the background was subsequently rebuilt when the line was electrified. (Photograph courtesy of the Lens Of Sutton Association)

An F5 hauled train waiting to leave Witham for Maldon: the F5s were the most common motive power for passenger trains until withdrawal in May 1958

F5 2-4-2T 67217 leaving Witham under the then A12 after bringing a goods train from Maldon on 9th May 1953 (G. R. Mortimer)

J15 65468 leaves Witham with the 9.50am for Maldon, Sunday 29 July 1957. Note the small goods platform on the left, now demolished
(G. R. Mortimer)

F5 67190 approaching Witham with train ex Maldon. Part of the extensive goods yard can be seen at the top of the photograph.
(R. E. Vincent, courtesy of The Transport Treasury)

A marvellously evocative photo of Witham with the branch locomotive running round its train on 17th March 1958
(Frank Church collection, courtesy of the Essex Bus Enthusiasts Group)

F5 67214 departing Witham for Maldon on 17th March 1958
(Frank Church collection, courtesy of the Essex Bus Enthusiasts Group)

J15 65470 at Witham, 10th May 1958. A J69 has just arrived from Maldon with it's passenger train
(R. C. Riley, courtesy of The Transport Treasury)

J69 68579 leaving Witham for Maldon (Dr. I. C. Allen, courtesy of The Transport Treasury)

This undated photograph from the railbus era shows a railbus arriving at Witham from Maldon: there were five of these German railbuses, built by Waggon und Maschinenbau (M. Harvey, courtesy of Maldon Museum)

Waggon und Maschinenbau railbus E79963 on the Maldon service, 5th October 1963 (Alec Swain, courtesy of The Transport Treasury)

The 4.50pm Witham to Maldon below the new A12 Witham by-pass bridge, Sunday 23rd August 1964 (G. R. Mortimer)

Witham Yard extended alongside the Maldon branch line, and was in use for some years after the closure of the branch. Here 31019 leaves the yard with one wagon and a brake van on 22nd February 1980 (Stephen Swingwood)

A failed 47233 of Cardiff awaiting rescue in Witham Yard, on the remains of the Maldon branch, 22nd August 1980
(Stephen Swingwood)

31112 waiting to shunt Witham Yard on 25th February 1981. The electric multiple unit is in the platform formerly used by the Maldon branch trains. (Stephen Swingwood)

Overbridge 14/872 at Witham on the Maldon branch on 7th December 1982 (Stephen Swingwood)

Shortly after leaving Witham for Maldon, the line crossed over the River Brain on a wooden trestle bridge, now demolished. This photograph by Frank Church, shows a J15, bunker first, pulling a Gresley coach in teak and a Thompson coach in carmine and cream

F5 67208, fitted with condensing gear, leaving Witham for Maldon. Whilst undated, this timeless view is believed to have been captured in the Fifties. (Dr. Ian C. Allan)

Wickham Bishops Station.

Pre-grouping view of Wickham Bishops, believed to be dating from around 1900: note the white painted wooden fence.
(Lens of Sutton Association)

This undated photo of Wickham Bishops shows the station house in a state of disrepair, and comes from the Maldon Museum collection

A relatively unusual arrangement applied at Wickham Bishops, whereby the single platform could only be accessed by crossing the loop line
(Stations UK)

J68 68666 (withdrawn in August 1958) approaching Wickham Bishops: note the hand-operated point lever for the siding (Dr. I. C. Allen)

Undated, but pre-1956, this view shows a three carriage train bound for Maldon
(D. Lawrence, courtesy of Photos From The Fifties)

F5 67195 leaving Wickham Bishops for Maldon in August 1957 (G. R. Mortimer)

Photographed from the road overbridge, 67214 approaches with a train from Witham to Maldon on April 21st 1958
(Frank Church, courtesy of the Essex Bus Enthusiasts Group)

This undated photograph of Wickham Bishops shows the hut beside the signal box, the siding and the platelayer's hut (Lens of Sutton)

J69 68573 (to be withdrawn in August 1960) at Wickham Bishops with a freight for Witham on 12th May 1958
(Frank Church, courtesy of the Essex Bus Enthusiasts Group)

A train of gas pipes passing through Wickham Bishops, undated (M. Harvey)

Another view of Wickham Bishops: the door on the right of the station buildings was the exit from the waiting room (Lens of Sutton)

Sundays only 2.50pm Witham to Maldon Metropolitan Cammell two car diesel unit eases into Wickham Bishops on 23rd August 1964. Mill House on the left was then lived in by the permanent way foreman of the line (G. R. Mortimer)

The 11.13 Maldon to Witham moves away from Wickham Bishops after one person boarded on 5th September 1964, the penultimate day of service. Note the absence of the signalbox, now demolished. A good view of Matthews Mill in the background (G.R. Mortimer)

Diesel railbus at Wickham Bishops in winter time, undated (Brian Stevens collection)

MALDON

A railbus with Driver Gordon Cottee at the controls crossing the trestle bridge at Wickham Bishops (M. Harvey)

The trestle bridge at WIckham Bishops just after the Great Storm of 1987: the gas pipe over the river has since been dismantled (Len Wilkinson)

This early 1950s photograph was taken from the road overbridge at Langford & Ulting Halt (Len Wilkinson collection)

The rather basic waiting shelter at Langford & Ulting in the mid 1950s (Lens of Sutton)

8.50am Witham to Maldon railbus passing through Langford & Ulting Halt on Saturday 5th September 1964: services finished the next day
(G.R. Mortimer)

This view of the imposing frontage of Maldon East station is undated (Lens of Sutton Association)

In the days before motor transport started to rule the world, steam power was present on the roads as well as the railways. Well known local Maldon firm John Sadd moved freight from Maldon East station to their premises with this traction engine
(Photograph courtesy of Essex Record Office)

Roof line detail at Maldon East: note the initials MWB (Maldon, WItham and Braintree Railway) and ECR (Eastern Counties Railway)

A freight train making its way up the siding which led down to the canal at Maldon
(Frank Church, courtesy of Essex Bus Enthusiasts Group)

A marvellous photograph of a subject rarely covered: the local permanent way gang in their Wickham trolley by the goods shed at Maldon East
(Len Wilkinson collection)

J69 68628 on a Railway Enthusiasts Club charter at Maldon East in April 1957 (Maldon Museum collection)

J15 65445 at Maldon East with a Witham train on 12th May 1958
(Frank Church, courtesy of the Essex Bus Enthusiasts Group)

An unidentified loco running round at Maldon East, with the goods shed to the left and the station to the right
(Frank Church, courtesy Essex Bus Enthusiasts Group)

The signalman at Maldon East prepares to receive the single line token as the 2.50pm ex Witham approaches the road crossing before the station area on 24th August 1964 (Jeff Morss)

The German railbuses did much for the economics of the line, with their reduced crewing costs, and did attract some new custom - but sadly insufficient to save the line. 79963 is seen here at Maldon East on 5th October 1963
(Alec Swain, courtesy of The Transport Treasury)

Bo-Bo D8220 approaching Maldon East with the 3.41pm from Witham: loco and three coaches deputising for a railcar due to it being Maldon Carnival day

(Frank Church, courtesy of Essex Bus Enthusiasts Group)

A Derby lightweight DMU at Maldon East station on 8th November 1960
(M. Harvey, courtesy of Maldon Museum)

Closing day, 15th April 1966, with D8202 shunting freight in light sleet (G. R. Mortimer)

This undated exterior view of the Goods Shed after closure comes from the Maldon Museum collection: the shed was demolished in 2009

This undated interior view of the Goods Shed at Maldon East after closure comes from the Maldon Museum collection

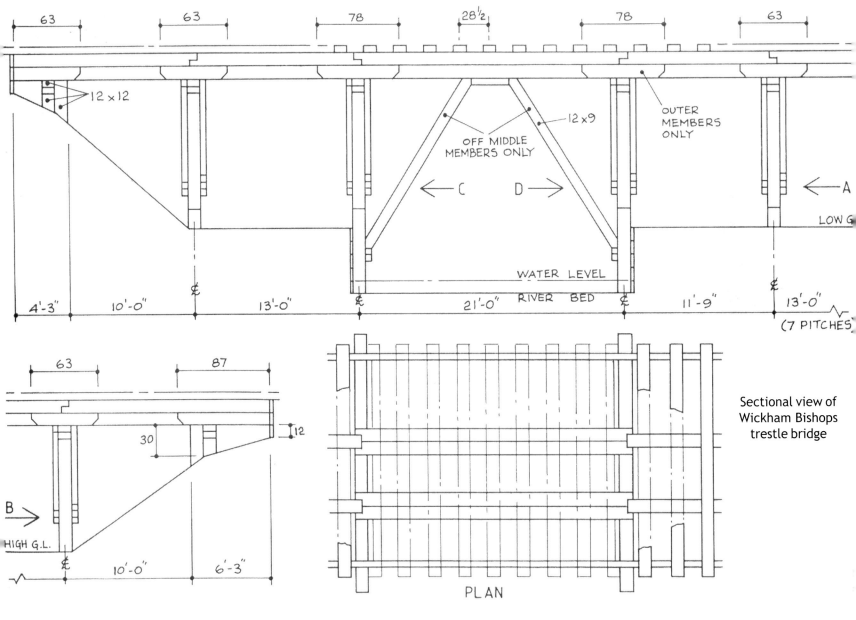

Sectional view of Wickham Bishops trestle bridge

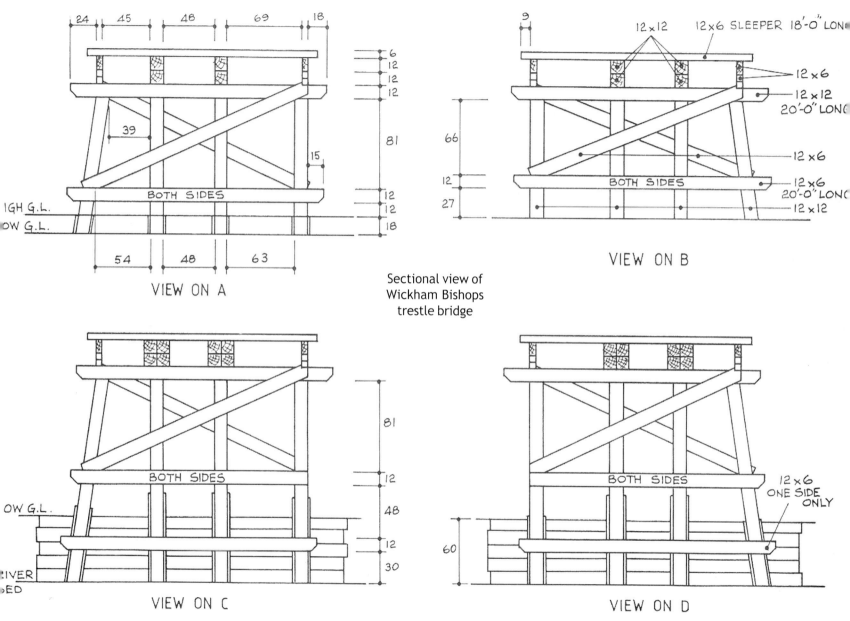

Sectional view of Wickham Bishops trestle bridge

VIEW ON A

VIEW ON B

VIEW ON C

VIEW ON D

A real train on the trestle bridge at Wickham Bishops

In an identical position to the previous photograph, this shows a train on the model layout

FRONT ELEVATION OF WICKHAM BISHOPS STATION HOUSE
AND WAITING ROOM LOOKING FROM PLATFORM

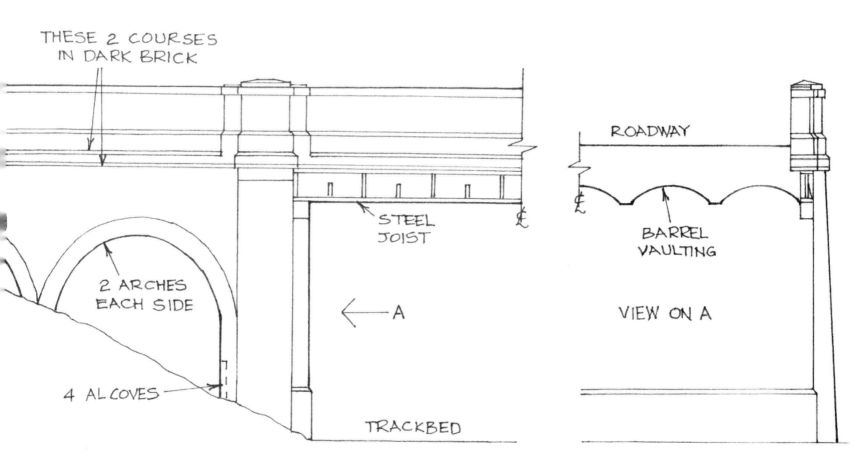

THESE 2 COURSES IN DARK BRICK

2 ARCHES EACH SIDE

4 ALCOVES

STEEL JOIST

← A

TRACKBED

ROADWAY

BARREL VAULTING

VIEW ON A

VIEWS OF SKEW ROAD BRIDGE AT WICKHAM BISHOPS
SHOWING INTRICATE DETAIL OF BRICK PIERS

THE MILL HOUSE. THE HOUSE WAS ORIGINALLY LIVED IN BY THE
FOREMAN OF THE LINE. THE SINGLE STOREY SECTION WAS THE STABLES

A view of the Wickham Bishops layout

Another view of the Wickham Bishops layout